The D* Theory of Consciousness & Mind

Alvin Richardson

Revive Publications

Copyright © 2011 by Alvin Richardson

All rights reserved. This book, or parts thereof, may not be reproduced in any form without permission.

A catalogue record for this book is available from the British Library

ISBN: 978-1-907962-40-0

Published by Revive Publications

Reading, England

For Marco

Contents

Preface		7
Introduction		9
1	The Big Bang	11
2	Can I Know Why I Feel?	19
3	The Distinctness of Consciousness & Mind	26
4	The Existing Theoretical Background	32
5	Toward a New Theory of D*	46
6	The D* Theory of Consciousness	53
7	Concluding Remarks	70
Bibliography		75

Preface

There are almost as many different views concerning the relationship between consciousness, mind, body, and world as there are people who think about the issue. Accordingly, a plethora of theories with many variants have been developed – these include supervenience, substance dualism, pansensism, occasionalism, epiphenomenalism, physicalism, panexperientialism, panpsychism, protophenomenalism, property dualism, and many others.

One might not think it useful to add another theory to this mix – the theory which I develop in this book and call D*. However, the fact that there are so many theories still supported surely means that none of these existing theories can be wholly convincing. So, there is some merit in exploring and developing (yet more!) new theories.

Introduction

It has long been held that consciousness is an attribute of the mind. In this book I question this long-held assumption and argue for a new theoretical framework in which consciousness is an attribute of the entire body rather than of the mind. I conclude that this new theory has much to commend it as it evades the main objections to both physicalism and panpsychism.

In *Chapter One* I start by considering the importance of the Big Bang to the relationship between consciousness, mind and body. In *Chapter Two* I consider whether I, or anyone else, can know why I feel. Then, in *Chapter Three,* I make the case for the distinctness of consciousness and mind. In *Chapter Four* I outline the existing positions relating to consciousness and mind. In the following two chapters – *Five* and *Six* – I develop the D* theory of consciousness. Finally in *Chapter Seven* I draw some conclusions.

Chapter 1

The Big Bang

For thousands of years humans have been contemplating their place in the universe. Two of the biggest questions they have tried to answer are: 'What is the relationship between my mind and my body?' And, 'What is consciousness?' Throughout this period there have been a multitude of attempts to answer these questions, attempts that have been inevitably informed and constrained by our best understanding of the universe prevailing at the time. The rapid scientific advancement in recent times means that today there is a much more rigid framework within which these two questions need to be addressed than at any time in the past.

One particular scientific advancement – the realization that the entire universe has slowly evolved from the singularity of the Big Bang – has very large implications for our attempts to understand consciousness and the mind-body relation. Anyone who accepts this well-established theory has also to accept that the fundamental constituents of reality that were in existence at the time of the Big Bang (the ultimates) are the very same constituents that comprise their own body. This means that when we contemplate our place in the universe we have to ask the question: 'Which attributes of a human are attributes of the ultimates of which a human is constituted?'

The Big Bang

In order to attempt to answer this question we need to identify the attributes of a human. It seems to me that there are four distinct groups of such attributes. The first attribute of a human is that it occupies space-time. The second attribute of a human is that it can reason and think. The third attribute of a human is that it has sensory qualities – it can hear, see, smell, taste and touch. The fourth and final attribute of a human is that it has feelings – we refer to these as such things as pains, aches, tickles, itches, tingles, pins-and-needles, emotions and moods.

Now that we have identified the attributes of a human we can return to our question: 'Which attributes of a human are attributes of the ultimates of which a human is constituted?' The dominant contemporary position (physicalism) asserts that the only attribute of a human that is an attribute of its constituent ultimates is that of space-time occupation; a human occupies space-time because its constituent ultimates occupy space-time. It is asserted that all of the other attributes of a human are not attributes of the ultimates.

Why does the physicalist separate out the attributes in this particular way? The reason is rooted in the mind-body problem. There has been a long-standing assumption that thinking, sensory and feeling attributes are all attributes of mind. Whilst a mind requires a brain, and thus requires space-time occupation, the rest of the body is seen as purely space-time occupation. The sole human attribute located in the body (excluding the brain) is the attribute of space-time occupation.

Where does consciousness fit into this picture? Consciousness is generally conceived of as being the fourth attribute – feelings. However, it is also assumed that consciousness is tightly linked to the second attribute – thinking, and the third attribute – sensory qualities. It is held that thinking can be conscious, and that sensory qualities can have a conscious feeling aspect. Consciousness is, therefore, considered to be involved in the three attributes of mind; it is considered to be a possible state of a mind. Consciousness, like mind, is seen as only entailing the first attribute – space-time occupation, because the mind-brain requires space-time occupation. In other words, in the mind-body debate, consciousness is seen as an attribute of mind, rather than of body. It follows that consciousness is a unique human attribute, and not an attribute of the ultimates out of which a human is constituted.

One might be tempted to wonder whether the division of the four attributes of a human carried out by the physicalist is an arbitrary one. Can one be certain that the physicalist has carved up reality in the right way? Can one be certain that the only attribute of a human which is an attribute of the ultimates of which it is constituted is space-time occupation? It seems that the main area of doubt is the fourth attribute – feelings. Could feelings be an attribute of ultimates rather than of humans? If so, the ultimate constituents of reality would have two attributes – space-time occupation, and feeling.

The Big Bang

Whilst the uniquely human attributes would be thinking and sensory qualities.

It is the objective of the rest of the book to ponder this possibility. Given that consciousness is so closely associated with feelings, if feelings are attributes of ultimates it seems that we will also have to assert that consciousness is an attribute of ultimates. If this is so we will need to consider the relationship between feeling space-time occupying ultimates and the unique human attributes of thinking and sensory qualities. We will also need to reconsider what a mind is. If all of reality is conscious then a mind is not what many consider it to be. It will be conscious, because it is composed of ultimates, but its only unique attribute will be thinking.

If feeling is an attribute of ultimates rather than of a human then we have a completely different vision of reality to the dominant contemporary view. But, is this so? We have to start by asking a simple question.

Chapter 2

Can I Know Why I Feel?

That I am a human and have feelings seems undeniable. We have seen that the physicalist carves up reality in such a way that these feelings are a unique human attribute rather than an attribute of the ultimates that constitute a human. How are we to judge whether this carving is correct? In other words: "Can I know why I feel?" There are, in fact, a number of positions that can account for my ability to feel.

One possibility is that my brain is made of a substance that doesn't feel, and my ability to feel arises from the existence of a second 'feeling' substance. This is a possibility; however, it sits very uncomfortably alongside our contemporary scientific worldview which, as we have seen, asserts a gradual evolution of the universe originating from the Big Bang. Accepting this theory means that substance dualism entails either a second substance coming into existence part-way through this process, which is hard to conceive, or that there were two distinct substances in existence at the time of the Big Bang, which seems improbable. So at a first glance, and for reasons of parsimony, the position of *ontological monism* seems to be a more likely candidate for a realistic description of reality.

So, what are the different ontological monist positions that could possibly explain my ability to feel? The first position, which I shall label A*, asserts that feelings are a higher-level property of my brain. The idea is that the ultimates that constitute my brain are totally devoid of feelings, but when they come together to form the structure that is my brain an emergence process occurs which gives rise to my feelings. The second position, which I shall call B*, asserts that feelings are a same-level property of my brain. The idea here is that the ultimates that constitute my brain are totally devoid of feelings, but when they come together to form the structure that is my brain then the matter of my brain has feelings. In contrast to A*, there is no need for emergence in B*, the matter of my brain itself just has feelings when it is in the structure that is my brain.

A third position, which I shall refer to as C*, asserts that I have feelings because there are cells in my brain. The idea here is that the ultimates that constitute my brain are totally devoid of feelings, but that they do not need to form a brain structure to generate feelings. In this position feelings are generated when ultimates come together to form cells. If C* explains my ability to feel, it means that not just every cell in my brain has feelings, but also that every cell in my body has feelings, and that every living thing has feelings. The fourth position, which I shall call D*, asserts that I have feelings because there are ultimates in my brain. There is no need for the ultimates to form cells, or my brain, for there to be feelings, the ultimates themselves are feeling. This is the position that earlier initiated our present pondering, and it leads to the conclusion that the whole universe is composed of space-occupying feeling ultimates.

These are the four ontological monist positions that could explain my ability to feel. How are we to decide which of them is the correct one? Or, if this is too much to ask, how are we to judge which of them is the most plausible description of reality?

Let us consider these various positions. A* and B* claim that a brain structure is necessary to generate feelings, C* and D* claim that this structure is not necessary, that the underpinning cells (C*) or ultimates (D*) are sufficient. As wherever there is a brain, or cells, they are composed of the ultimates of D*, there is no way to refute D* by arguing for A*, B* or C*. All of these 3 positions are "dependent" on the ultimates of D*. So, there is no way that I could possibly tell if my feelings are in the ultimates themselves irregardless of their present location in my brain, or whether I only have feelings because the ultimates are currently arranged into the structure that is my brain.

So, to summarize, I have suggested that a type of ontological monism is the most likely description of reality. However, within this paradigm there seem to be four distinct positions which can explain why I have feelings. It is here that we seem to hit a logical wall. It could be argued that my ability to feel results from having a brain, but wherever there is a brain it will be composed of matter. This means that there is no possible way for me to judge in any serious and logical manner whether my feelings arise from my

Can I Know Why I Feel?

brain (A* or B*) or from the matter that pervades my whole body (D*). It certainly seems to me that every corner of my body can be filled with feeling states - I have pains *in* my fingers, aches *in* my stomach, pins and needles *in* my legs, and moods and emotions which seem to fill every crevice of my body. This all seems to support the assertion that feelings are not dependent on my brain (C* or D*). However, this is a mere seeming and not a wholly decisive argument. It seems that any of the four positions could be true. What *is* certain is that position D* - that matter itself has feelings - is a serious possibility.

Chapter 3

The Distinctness of Consciousness and Mind

I started this book by posing two questions that humans have been trying to answer for thousands of years: 'What is the relationship between my mind and my body?' And, 'What is consciousness?' I have asserted that I think and I feel, and I assume that any human who ponders the nature of their existence would assert the same things. I take it that the reason a person would assert that they have a 'mind' is that they undergo what I have described as 'thinking.' Having a 'mind' is simply the ability to think. It is naturally assumed that thinking occurs in

The Distinctness of Consciousness and Mind

the brain, and not throughout the entire body, so we have a division between the 'mind' and the 'body'. This doesn't seem to be that mysterious; the mind is simply the part of the body that thinks.

I have described the relationship between the mind and the body in such a way that one could be tempted to respond: "That all seems very obvious, why have people been debating it for thousands of years?" The answer to this question seems to be that the way I have described the mind (the thinking part of the body) is *not* the way that most people conceive of the mind. In fact for thousands of years people have generally held that a mind is not something that just thinks; it is also something that is conscious. It is this notion of consciousness and how it is related to mind and body that is the real bone of contention. For me, the assertion that I am conscious means nothing more than the assertion that I have feelings. Some people like to oppose 'being conscious' with 'being unconscious,' but this is simply an assertion that *when* I am not unconscious I am *aware* that I have feelings. Others like to suppose that 'being conscious' has some sort of relationship to 'information access,' when this is actually just an assertion that *when* I remember things I *also* have feelings. Let us accept that the most sensible answer to the question: 'What is consciousness?', is, simply: 'To have feelings.' After all, *if* I was devoid of feelings I would be a non-conscious mythical creature called a 'zombie.'

In other words, I am claiming that to think is to have a mind, and that to be conscious is to have feelings. Furthermore, I am asserting that there has been a long-standing assumption that when we ask the questions – 'What is the relationship between my mind and my body?' and, 'What is consciousness?' – that the property of consciousness has been assumed to be an attribute of mind rather than an attribute of the body. This doesn't seem that unreasonable as whenever we think, we are also conscious. However, as we have seen, we have no good logical reasons for assuming that consciousness is an attribute of the brain/mind (A* or B*), rather than of the body (C* or D*). This means that it is entirely possible that thinking *isn't* a conscious process; it is just something that occurs in a body that *is* composed of matter that is conscious.

So, I am proposing that in my quest to understand why I have feelings, and why I have the particular feelings that I do, that it is entirely coherent to argue that the real issue of concern might not be the relationship between my mind and my body. It might, instead, be the relationship between my feelings (consciousness) and my body. This is an acceptable position to take because we have seen that we are unable to make any logical headway with the assertion that my feelings are linked to my brain (A* or B*) rather than my body (C* or D*). And I have defined the mind as the thought processes that occur in the brain, so my feelings would arise from my body rather than my mind if C* or D* were true.

The Distinctness of Consciousness and Mind

In other words, arguing that mind and consciousness are two distinct things is a coherent position. However, the long-held assumption that minds *are* conscious things means that there is a lack of a theoretical framework to describe what this actually means in practice. Without a theoretical framework it is very hard to assess the possibility that my feelings result from C* or D*, rather than A* or B*. It is such a theoretical framework that I hope to provide the foundations for in the rest of the book.

Chapter 4

The Existing Theoretical Background

Their widespread attribution of the property of consciousness to the mind rather than the body makes the existing theoretical frameworks incapable of handling the distinctness of consciousness and mind. In the literature the position that I have called A* has several variants; two of the most popular are functionalism and supervenience. The position I have called B* is referred to as the mind-brain identity theory. All of these theories in assuming that a mind is a conscious thing just seek to explain

The Existing Theoretical Background

one thing: how does mind/consciousness relate to the brain. In contrast, I am asserting that there are *two things* that need explanation: the relation of mind to brain, *and* the relation between body and consciousness.

There are obvious links between the positions I have labelled C* and D*, and the existing theoretical work on a position called panpsychism. To recap, C* asserts that all living cells are conscious, whilst D* asserts that all matter is conscious. It should also be recalled that both of these positions distinguish consciousness from mind. The position of panpsychism asserts that mind is a fundamental feature of reality that exists throughout the universe. There are many variants of this position, but we can characterize it in general as asserting that all matter has mind

- there is no such thing as matter totally devoid of mind. It is worth spending some time describing how this position differs from C* and D*, so that we are clear about why the existing framework of panpsychism is inadequate for assessing the merits of these two positions.

Many people have been drawn to panpsychism because they consider the alternative, that mind arises out of matter that is totally devoid of mind, as unpalatable. There has thus been considerable debate over the question of emergence: some hold that mind can arise out of matter that is wholly devoid of mind, whilst others hold that all matter must itself possess mind. These have been considered to be the two alternative positions that one can hold - one must be either an emergentist or a panpsychist.

It seems to me that the intuitions that have drawn so many people to panpsychism have not been totally unfounded. However, it is also obvious why so many people should find the position bordering on the ridiculous. The panpsychist has one of two routes that he can go down. He can be a 'strong panpsychist' and assert that the nature of mind in a stone is the same as that in a human mind. It is this position that Colin McGinn finds "ludicrous,"[i] as it entails that "neurons in my brain literally feel pain, see yellow, think about dinner-and so do electrons and stars."[ii] This seems to be a fair point and is the reason why, in their bid for respectability, panpsychists have always gravitated towards 'weak panpsychism'. This position asserts that the quality of mind in a human is at a high level, and other parts of reality have differing amounts of a lesser quality of mind. So, Ervin Laszlo asserts that: "[we do not claim that] psyche is present throughout reality in the same way, at the same level of development. We say that psyche evolves, the same as matter."[iii] Whilst, Galen Strawson concludes that: "we will have to wonder how macroexperientiality arises from microexperientiality."[iv]

This attribution of differing qualities of mind to different parts of reality by the weak panpsychist is justified by the notion of 'analogical extension'. We observe the world around us and look for creatures that look and act similar to the way we do, and that ideally also have a similar genetic structure and

The Existing Theoretical Background

evolutionary history. If the similarities between them and us are high then we are supposedly justified in extending mind to such creatures by analogy. This may seem harmless enough, and seems intuitively like a very appropriate thing to do. However, it seems to me that the weak panpsychist can easily get himself into great difficulties through the use of analogical extension. The method starts off okay, it seems reasonable to attribute a slightly lesser quality mind to a chimpanzee than a human, a lesser quality mind to a dog than a chimpanzee, then a lesser quality mind still to a flee. But who is seriously going to believe that this method can reach the endpoint that the weak panpsychist aims for - that there are sufficient similarities between a human and a quark to extend mind to the quark by analogy. Even though the quality of mind attributed is now incomparably inferior to that of a human, this attribution by analogy seems fanciful to say the least.

Let us sharpen up our terminology a little. Both the weak panpsychist and the strong panpsychist seek to attribute mind to the fundamental physical attributes of reality; we can refer to these attributes as 'ultimates'. The weak panpsychist asserts that these ultimates have a quality of mind that is far inferior to a human mind. He thus owes us an explanation of how these inferior minds can combine in a meaningful way to produce a superior human mind. This is known as the panpsychist 'combination problem', and no remotely satisfactory solution to this problem has yet been formulated. In contrast, the strong panpsychist seeks to persuade us that the quality of mind in ultimates is on a par with humans. If a human mind is even remotely linked to a brain then this is surely a hopeless task.

Given the seemingly hopeless nature of the task facing the strong panpsychist, a coherent panpsychist position seems to depend on weak panpsychism - we would need to accept that there is a sliding scale of mindedness and find a solution to the 'combination problem'. Of course, the long-standing assumption that consciousness is an attribute of mind has led some weak panpsychists to describe their analogical extension in terms of feelings or consciousness, rather than mind. However, as far as they are concerned they *are* also extending mind, because for them consciousness *is* mind.

It should now be clear why the existing theoretical framework of panpsychism is unable to handle the distinctness of consciousness and mind. In attempting to assess the likelihood that my feelings are explicable by D* I cannot resort to panpsychism because panpsychism doesn't acknowledge the distinctness in the first place. What it *does* propose, instead, is that there is a 'sliding scale' of the *oneness* that is consciousness/mind. So, it is clear that D* is not a variant of panpsychism. However, *if* D* were true, it would explain why so many people have been drawn to panpsychism over the past two thousand years.

I propose that if we are looking for a coherent and logical theory there are numerous good reasons for preferring D* over both panpsychism and physicalism. To recapitulate, the appeal of panpsychism is that one doesn't inherit the physicalist 'emergence problem' of explaining how mind could arise out of matter wholly devoid of mind. Given that the panpsychist sees feelings as an attribute of mind, this physicalist problem can be expressed more persuasively as the problem of giving a convincing account of how something that feels could possibly arise out of something that is totally devoid of feeling. Escaping this problem is the attraction of panpsychism. However, we have seen that by equating feelings and mind the panpsychist faces the seeming absurdity of strong panpsychism, or the 'combination problem' of weak panpsychism. It isn't clear which of these two problems is actually the most insoluble - the physicalist 'emergence problem' or the panpsychist 'combination problem.' The advantage of D* is that evades *both* of these problems.

How can this be so? Well, by distinguishing consciousness from mind, D* enables us to coherently assert what the strong panpsychist would love to do, but is unable to do. D* theorists can assert that the consciousness/feelings in an electron are *not* of an inferior quality to the feelings in me; whilst, concordantly asserting that there is no such thing as a mind in an electron. In this way we don't have to worry about McGinn's objection that an electron would have to be "thinking about dinner" in the same way as a human. By being able to embrace the aspect of strong panpsychism that relates to feelings, D* theory escapes having to give a solution to the 'combination problem'. This is because the weak panpsychist assumption that ultimates have inferior feelings which somehow need to be combined into superior human feelings is rejected. Of course, an account of how the mind emerges, and a detailed account of how human experience appears to be so unified will also be sought by the D* theorist. However, this problem is called the 'binding problem', and it is a very different animal to the 'combination problem.' The 'binding problem' is faced in equal measure by *all* ontological monists, and seems to be far less problematic.

It should already be clear how the D* theorist also evades the physicalist 'emergence problem'. In accepting that the feelings in an electron are not inferior to the feelings in me, the D* theorist can simply expand this claim and assert that this also applies universally: there is no reason to assert that the feelings in the ultimates in me are of a superior quality to the feelings in ultimates in any other part of the universe, and this will apply back to the origin of the universe. It is in order to evade the 'emergence problem', and thus to provide a coherent and logical account of reality, that I have stopped referring to C*. An allegiance to C* would still leave one with this difficult problem. I will from now on just refer to the feasibility of D* as an account of my feelings.

A further advantage of D* is that it can give a much more plausible account of 'analogical extension'. It can be claimed that what should be extended by analogy is only mind and not consciousness. The notion that consciousness could be analogically extended would be seriously mistaken; we shouldn't talk about a sliding scale of consciousness. Of course when it comes to mind analogical extension would seem to be entirely appropriate. In this way the D* theorist evades the dubious claim of the weak panpsychist that the mind of a human is analogous to the mind of a quark; for the D* theorist there is no mind in a quark.

Chapter 5

Toward a New Theory of D*

The advantages of D* are obvious. However, one might be tempted to respond to the theory: "The assertion that an electron could have feelings of an equal quality to me is patently as implausible as the notion that an electron is thinking about dinner." The aim of this section is to try and explain why this response is misplaced, although understandable. My hope is that after I have laid out the theoretical framework for D* that one will also be prepared to accept the stronger claim that: "I have every reason to believe that other parts of reality could have feelings that are of a greater quality than those in me."

As a theory that asserts that there is a distinctness between consciousness and mind, the theoretical framework of D* needs to incorporate both the relation of mind to brain, *and* the relation between body and consciousness. There are, of course, a plethora of theories that attempt to explain the first of these relations, how the mind relates to the brain. Of course, all of these theories, in accepting that feelings are an attribute of mind, seek to explain *both* what I have defined as feeling *and* thinking. As far as the D* theorist is concerned these theories can only ever be successful at arriving at the true nature of the relationship between thinking and the brain. Whatever claims an A* theorist or a B* theorist might make concerning feelings, the D* theorist will reject, and respond that it is just a theory of mind and not a theory of consciousness.

What this means is that in order to establish the validity of the theory, a D* theorist does *not* actually have to give an account of the relationship between mind and brain. A D* theorist will be happy to accept *whichever* account of this relation eventually turns out to be the correct one. The onus on the D* theorist is to convince the A* theorist and the B* theorist that their accounts do not address the issue of consciousness. They need to be convinced of *why* a *second* account is required - an account of the relationship between body and consciousness.

Toward a New Theory of D*

In order to set the groundwork for the D* theoretical framework of consciousness it is helpful to start with the notion of a quale. These hypothesized entities are the subject of great debate, and as far as the D* theorist is concerned the main reason why people conflate mind and consciousness, when they are in fact distinct things. A quale is a term that is used to define a given conscious experience. The quale believers assert that when I view a red tomato I am in possession of a 'red quale,' that when I view a quail I am in possession of a 'quail quale', and that when I hear the musical note Middle C that I am in possession of a 'Middle C quale'. These things are supposedly *conscious* experiences with a given qualitative nature. There is hypothesized to be something that 'it is like' for me to see a red tomato, this experience is supposedly a conscious event.

Some people believe that these qualia exist and some deny it. What is our D* theorist to make of them? He will surely assert that they don't exist, that consciousness is purely about feelings, and there isn't anything that exists that is a *specific* feeling associated with viewing a quail - the hypothesized 'quail quale'. The viewing of the quail as a mental event would need to be distinguished from the feelings that are pertaining in the body at the time the quail is viewed. It is when these two things are run-together, and it is assumed that the mental viewing has a tightly associated conscious quale, that it seems that consciousness and the mind are one and the same thing.

Toward a New Theory of D*

All that is involved in viewing a colour, or a bird, or listening to a musical note, is a set of repetitive objective processes. Whenever a very limited number of physical states are present, the outcome, whether it be the creation of a colour, or the registering of a sound, will be the same. This is the mental aspect - part of the relation between the mind and the brain. For these repetitive objective processes to also be conscious processes there would need to be an associated conscious quale that ceaselessly exists whenever the objective process occurs. There needs to be something that it feels like to see red that is an identical feeling *every* time I see red. It is this whole story that the D* theorist finds highly implausible.

It is surely possible that the feelings associated with seeing a red tomato at t, could be very different from the feelings associated with seeing the tomato at t_{+1}. It also seems that there could be no feeling whatsoever associated with seeing the tomato at t_{+2}. However, on all of these occasions exactly the same quality of 'redness' is created. If this is what someone wants to call a 'red quale' then they should at least accept that it has no relationship to consciousness. We should conclude that there is no direct relationship between these objective processes and our feelings.

Chapter 6

The D* Theory of Consciousness

Having dispatched 'conscious' qualia it is time to outline the D* theoretical framework of consciousness. It should be remembered that the assertion of the D* theorist is that the reason that I have feelings is that the ultimates that compose my body are having feelings. It naturally follows that all of the ultimates in the universe can be argued to also have feelings. This means that an account of consciousness, of *why* certain ultimates feel one way, rather than another way, will obviously not have sense organs as a central component. After all, the entire universe is hypothesized to be in a state of feeling, and only a tiny part of the universe has sense organs.

The D* theoretical framework of consciousness will be centered on the ultimate constituents of reality and their interactions with other ultimates. The most natural position for a D* theorist to take would entail two simple assertions: A) Every ultimate constituent of reality has an intrinsic feeling state; B) Every physical interaction between ultimates will result in a change in this intrinsic feeling state. It would be an open question, and obviously an unanswerable one, whether at the origin of the universe every ultimate had a unique feeling state, or a homogenous feeling state. However, it would follow from B) that even if the initial state was homogenous, then almost immediately this state would be modified by physical interactions.

In other words, the D* theorist can assert that for every single physical interaction in the universe that occurs, and has ever occurred, there is an associated feeling state. Of course, one might be tempted to assert that the physical interactions *themselves* can give a perfectly good account of reality without postulating associated feeling states. But this seems to be obviously false, because it is precisely the existence of my feeling states that physics is unable to explain. It will be helpful to describe a range of physical interactions in detail and how the D* theorist conceives of the associated changes in feeling.

Consciousness & Mind

There are, of course, a diverse range of physical interactions in the world, and this means that there will be different mechanisms that initiate changes in feeling states. These changes in feeling states will vary greatly in duration from the fleeting to the long-term. It must be remembered when discussing these states that the D* theorist asserts that at all times the feeling states themselves are wholly felt by ultimates. For ease of expression it is useful to refer to the feeling in an 'atom', but what this actually means is: "the feelings in the ultimates in the area of space-time filled by an atom."

The first set of physical interactions lead to long-term feeling changes. A prime example of these interactions is chemical reactions and sub-atomic physical interactions. So we can consider a simple chemical reaction in which the elements hydrogen and oxygen react together to form the chemical compound water. A D* theorist would assert that this reaction entails different feeling entities coming together in such a way as to create a new feeling state.

Furthermore, we can compare the physical structure of a hydrogen atom itself to that of a sodium atom, and when we do so we find great differences. A hydrogen atom is comprised of a nucleus containing a single proton, in addition to a single orbiting electron. In contrast, a sodium atom is comprised of a nucleus containing 11 protons and 12 neutrons, and has 11 orbiting electrons. A D* theorist will assert that protons, neutrons, and electrons will all have different feeling states

Consciousness & Mind

themselves. This means that the area of space-time occupied by a hydrogen atom will contain a very different feeling to that area of space-time occupied by a sodium atom. Atoms can be thought of as long-term "feeling associations" – the individual feeling nature of the electrons, neutrons, and protons, and the way they interact together, produces a particular feeling state in a particular area of space-time.

The second set of physical interactions will be those that lead to transitory feeling effects. In these cases two physical entities come into contact with each other only momentarily and then part again with their original feeling state still intact. An example of this would be say, a sandstorm, in which the grains of sand have fleeting feeling interactions with neighboring grains as they fly into both each other and the ground below. Another example would be a person running a marathon; this would entail a multitude of transitory feeling interactions between the soles of their trainers and the ground.

A third set of physical interactions which are worth differentiating from the others are physical waves. When a material body comes into contact with a physical wave there will be a feeling interaction that affects them both. Whilst a brief interaction would seem to entail only a transitory feeling effect, it seems that a prolonged interaction could change the feeling state of a material body quite considerably. Of course, the magnitude of the changes in feeling would also seem to be dependent on the type of interacting wave. A radio wave has a wavelength of several meters, whilst a light wave has a wavelength of approximately a hundred thousandth of a centimeter. This means that light waves will have much more energy, and this could very possibly mean that an interaction with a light wave will entail a much greater change in feeling than an interaction with a radio wave.

We can now attempt to describe the factors that will determine the state of feeling in my body at a particular moment in time. My body itself is composed of a plethora of atoms, molecules and cells that as we have seen are themselves long-term "feeling associations" which incorporate the individual feeling nature of various electrons, neutrons, and protons, and their interactions, in a particular area of space-time. When we look at my body as a whole we surely have to conclude, given that the feelings are in the ultimates themselves, that there are no absolute boundaries *between* "feeling associations". Rather, my body is a flux of an immense number of different *overlapping* "feeling associations". The longer that particular ultimates have been in my body the greater the number of these associations that they will be a part of, whilst an ultimate that has a speedy journey through my body won't have much of a chance to interact with, and form associations with, the surrounding ultimates. Of course, the skin of my body won't be a barrier to such interactions. I wear the same pair of spectacles for 16 hours a day, so the ultimates in my nose and ears will be part of "feeling associations" that include the ultimates in my spectacles.

It is these "feeling associations" of the ultimates in my body that is the bedrock of the feelings I am aware of in my body. These associations are always being changed by external stimuli, and 'external' in this sense makes no reference to the boundary of my body. My feelings are modified by a plethora of things: the food and drink that I have recently, and not so recently, consumed; the molecule entering my nasal passage; the mechanical vibrations that interact with my entire body and which are interpreted by my ears as sound; the transitory changes of consciousness resulting from my tapping the table with my fingers; light waves interacting with the ultimates in my body, including those entering my eyes. And it doesn't stop there, there will also be bodily feeling changes resulting from the gravitational effects of the Moon as it revolves around the Earth, affecting the ultimates in my body just as certainly as the ultimates in the oceans that are physically moved by it to cause our tides. Of course, an appreciation that all of the matter in the universe exerts a gravitational force on all other matter leads to the conclusion that my bodily feelings would also be affected, however slightly, by every material body in the universe.

How will these physical-feeling interactions in my body compare to those in a stone? Of course, the D* theorist is committed to the view that the conscious interactions in my body are not necessarily of a superior quality to those in a stone. We can now see clearly how this makes perfect sense - conscious interactions are just interactions between ultimates, and there is no reason to assert that there is any fundamental difference between an interaction between two ultimates in a stone *vis-à-vis* a human body. Given this, the coherence of my previous 'stronger claim' also becomes clear. This was the claim that: "I have every reason to believe that other parts of reality could have feelings that are of a greater quality than those in me." If a feeling state is generated by the interactions between two ultimates, why shouldn't one assert that there could be interactions that occur outside a human body that generate a feeling state of greater quality than those that occur inside a human body?

A live candidate for a conscious state of greater quality than that in a human would be that pertaining during radioactive decay. The radium atoms in the chemical compound radium bromide can spontaneously tear themselves apart and break down into radon and helium atoms. This is a process that entails a very large energy output, and there seems to be no reason why the feeling state that it entails couldn't be immensely greater than any feeling a human has ever, or could ever, experience.

One might be tempted to object that there surely are feelings in a human that are uniquely human, feelings which are of a superior quality to those in the rest of nature. After all, humans can love, have a state of extreme ecstasy, feel excruciating pain, and feel remorseless depression. If we find ourselves tempted by this objection we simply need to remind ourselves that humans have a mind which enables them to give labels to their feelings; the vast majority of the universe has feelings but it does not have a mind. It is entirely natural that if you have a mind that you should try and give labels to a very vague type of feeling that you are aware of in your body, in this way you can attempt to communicate your feelings to others. However, we do really need to admit that when we talk about our human feelings, emotions, and moods, we are just attaching a 'label' to a very vague feeling residing in "feeling associations" of ultimates. There really is no specific state of feeling that is "pain" or "ecstasy". There is just an unimaginably large number of incredibly diverse "feeling associations" in the universe. Some of these are wholly or partially located in a human body, and it is to some of these that a human will typically try and attach a 'label'.

The D* Theory of Consciousness

Having said this, the D* theorist has a good argument as to why the *diversity* and *richness* of consciousness in a human body will be infinitely greater than that in a stone, even if the feeling interactions in the two are of exactly the same quality. Firstly, we can look at the number of known elements. We would expect *ceteris paribus* that areas of space-time that contain relatively few of these elements would have far fewer feeling states than a comparable area of space-time with a great abundance of elements. Secondly, we would expect that an area of space-time with a great number and diversity of interactions would have a greater number of associated feeling states than a comparable area of space-time with far fewer of these interactions. As it turns out a human body is fairly unique, it fills a comparatively small area, but is both exceptionally complex, and nearly all of the known elements have already been identified within it. So, when considering both the composition *and* great physical complexity of the human body, a D* theorist would expect that there is a greater diversity and richness of conscious states there than in any other known part of reality of a comparable size.

Given the immense number of physical forces continuously modifying the state of consciousness within my body, it seems that there are very compelling grounds for supposing that my body can never ever be in the same state of consciousness again that it is in at the present moment. My consciousness isn't describable in terms of qualia, it is these all-pervading forces that determine my consciousness, and distinguish it from my mind.

Chapter 7

Concluding Remarks

I have started from the knowledge of my own feeling states and sought to work out what I can logically know about how they are related to by body, brain, and mind. It was soon realized that very little headway could actually be made on purely logical grounds because there are four different equally plausible explanations - A*, B*, C* and D*. I was therefore forced to conclude that that it is possible that my feeling states could be distinct from my brain; that it is plausible that consciousness and mind are two distinct things.

Concluding Remarks

In exploring the existing theoretical frameworks of consciousness/mind, particularly that of panpsychism, it became clear that a new theoretical framework was required. It is impossible to assess the plausibility of a theory that asserts the distinctness of consciousness and mind within frameworks that don't accept such a distinction.

I hope that I have succeeded in putting forward the case for the theory of D^* - the theory that mind and consciousness are distinct - in a coherent and compelling manner. By asserting that mind emerges but that consciousness doesn't, it is a theory that evades the major problems faced by both physicalism and panpsychism. However, my only aim has been to try and argue that D^* is at least a remotely plausible candidate for an accurate description of reality.

Bibliography

---

[i] Colin McGinn, *The Mysterious Flame*, (New York: Basic Books, 1999), p.97.

[ii] Colin McGinn, *The Mysterious Flame*, (New York: Basic Books, 1999), p.96.

[iii] Ervin Laszlo, *Science and the Akashic Field*, (Vermont, Inner Traditions, 2004), p.147.

[iv] Galen Strawson, *Consciousness and its place in nature*, (Exeter: Imprint Academic, 2006), p.26.

www.ingramcontent.com/pod-product-compliance
Lightning Source LLC
Chambersburg PA
CBHW071411040426
42444CB00009B/2194